Original title: Glimpses of Infinity

Author: Olivia Orav
Editor: Jessica Elisabeth Luik
ISBN 978-9916-39-969-9

Glimpses of Infinity

Olivia Orav

Endless Allure

In twilight's soft embrace,
Where whispers fill the air,
A dreamer's heart will race,
With shadows light and fair.

The stars above will gleam,
On paths we dare to tread,
Each moment feels a dream,
In endless allure spread.

Through valleys deep and wide,
The night does gently sway,
With secrets time can't hide,
That lure us far away.

Unbounded Realms

In realms where freedom reigns,
Unshackled, wild, and free,
The soul no longer strains,
It dances, joyously.

Mountains kiss the skies,
Rivers carve their path,
With wonder in our eyes,
We witness nature's wrath.

Horizons ever vast,
No borders to confine,
We journey till the last,
Through realms of the divine.

Infinite Reverie

In dreams we softly roam,
Through landscapes vast and wide,
Each heart finds a new home,
Where limitless thoughts reside.

A symphony of stars,
Guides us on our way,
Past Jupiter and Mars,
Through night into the day.

Imagination's spark,
Ignites the soul's delight,
In reveries so stark,
We soar beyond the night.

Beyond Time's Grasp

A timeless whisper calls,
Beyond the grasp of years,
Through ancient, hallowed halls,
Is heard by listening ears.

The sands of time do slip,
Yet we remain in grace,
On this eternal trip,
Through endless time and space.

Moments blend and blur,
Yet love and memories last,
In heartbeats we confer,
Our tales beyond time's grasp.

Endless Tapestry

Threads of gold in twilight's loom,
Whispers woven soft as plumes.
Colors blend in night's embrace,
Patterns form a timeless space.

Through the ages, tales unfold,
Memories in fabric old.
Dreams we dream, a silent cry,
Woven 'neath the starry sky.

Every stitch, a heartbeat's call,
Captured moments, free for all.
In the weave of life and lore,
One can feel the spirits soar.

Echoes in Eternity

In the halls of endless time,
Chimes of ages softly chime.
Voices lost in shadows vast,
Whisper secrets from the past.

Through the veils of what once was,
Echos sing just because.
Silent words of love and pain,
Trace the path of endless gain.

Moments flicker, fade, and glow,
Joining hands with those we know.
In the echoes, truth is found,
Circling eternity's bound.

The Eternal Labyrinth

Winding paths in darkness deep,
Secrets that the shadows keep.
Turn and twist through endless maze,
Lost within the twilight's gaze.

Journey through the unseen door,
Steps that echo evermore.
Labyrinth of mind and heart,
Where the end becomes the start.

Every corner, every bend,
Promises the journey's end.
Yet within this tangled trace,
Truth resides in every place.

Unraveling the Infinite

Threads of stars in cosmic sea,
Weave the vast infinity.
Galaxies like pearls aligned,
In the fabric of the mind.

Mysteries in light profound,
Orbit in a silent sound.
Unraveling the endless thread,
Of the universe widespread.

Boundless skies and voids unknown,
In the infinite we're shown.
Journey through the space and time,
Seek the endless in the rhyme.

Eternal Whispers

In twilight's gentle, quiet grace,
A whisper sails through time and space,
Echoes weave through nights and days,
Tales of love in silent praise.

Stars dance with ancient lore,
Whispers linger, ask for more,
Moonlight bathes the listening ear,
Eternal whispers always near.

In dreams we find their tender call,
Guiding souls through shadows' fall,
Secrets shared in softest tongue,
Forever old, forever young.

Boundless Reflections

In mirrored lakes, the skies unfold,
A canvas vast in twilight's hold,
Waves reflect the endless dreams,
In boundless, silent, liquid beams.

Through glassy eyes, we find the past,
Shadows cast from light's last blast,
Moments flicker, fade, and blend,
Reflections where horizons end.

Infinite echoes in each wave,
Timeless truths the waters crave,
In this dance, both lost and found,
Whispered truths in silence bound.

The Infinite Trail

Steps imprint the sands of time,
Paths that weave through space and rhyme,
Footprints left in nature's tale,
Following the infinite trail.

Winds whisper where we tread,
Stories of the lost and led,
Through forests thick, by rivers wide,
On this path, there's naught to hide.

Stars above our guiding light,
Through the vast and endless night,
Every journey, every stride,
Bound by trails where dreams reside.

Fragments of the Eternal

Shattered echoes of the past,
Fragments in the shadows cast,
Pieces of the timeless lore,
Scattered in the evermore.

In each shard, a story lives,
Memories the silence gives,
Threads of fate in delicate lace,
Woven through both time and space.

Whole within the fractured few,
Truths that shine both old and new,
In these glimpses, brief and rare,
Fragments of the eternal share.

Echoes in Eternity

Whispers of the past, gently intertwine,
In the corridors of time, memories align.
Echoes resonate, in silent symphony,
A dance of moments, through eternity.

Shadows fade but never truly depart,
Carved in the essence of a timeless heart.
Infinity cradles each fleeting glance,
In endless loops, we waltz the trance.

Stars immortal cast their ancient glow,
Revealing mysteries we yearn to know.
In every heartbeat, in every sigh,
Echoes of existence, never say goodbye.

Boundless Dreams

In realms untamed, where visions soar,
Our boundless dreams forever explore.
Unchained by night, unburdened by day,
In the canvas of sleep, we find our way.

Seas of wonder, skies profound,
In boundless dreams, we are unbound.
Endless horizons, spirits take flight,
In star-lit journeys through velvet night.

Through shadowed paths and radiant gleams,
We chase the whisper of boundless dreams.
In silent realms where fantasies gleam,
We find our truth beneath the moonbeam.

Unveiling the Infinite

Dew-kissed dawn unveils the sky,
In hues of wonder, our souls comply.
Boundaries vanish in morning light,
Infinite vistas in our sight.

The whispering winds tell ancient tales,
Unveiling secrets where mystery prevails.
We sail on dreams through the cosmic haze,
Guided by stars, in the endless maze.

Moments converge in space so vast,
Present, future, meld with the past.
In the heart of the infinite, we roam,
Discovering places we call home.

Eternal Visions

Glimmers of light in an endless sea,
Eternal visions come to be.
Within the void, our souls ignite,
Dreams and reality reunite.

In the cradle of the stars we lie,
Beneath the sweeping cosmic sky.
Timeless echoes call us home,
To realms where endless spirits roam.

Eternal visions weave our fate,
In love and awe, we contemplate.
Through silent night and radiant dawn,
In the web of existence, we are drawn.

Eternal Murmurs

Whispers of dawn in the gentle breeze,
Awakened hearts from their sleep arise.
Ancient echoes through the trees,
Resonate in the azure skies.

Mountains stand, eternal guards,
Witnesses of countless dreams.
Streams speak in hushed regards,
Their murmurs carry silent beams.

Stars align with whispered lore,
Murmurs of the night unfold.
Mysteries that time implored,
In the cosmos, secrets told.

Timeless Footprints

Footprints etched in golden sands,
Trace the paths of days gone by.
Moments held by unseen hands,
Beneath the ever-watching sky.

Waves of time in endless dance,
Erase the fleeting marks we leave.
Yet memories of each chance,
In hearts and souls eternally weave.

Footsteps of the past remain,
Shadowed by the setting sun.
In the echoes still we gain,
A glimpse of all that's just begun.

Infinite Wanderings

Journeys through the vast unknown,
Guided by a distant light.
In the heart of lands unshown,
Wanderers embrace the night.

Steps that lead through realms of dreams,
Boundless paths of endless sky.
Rivers flow with crystal gleams,
Infinite, they wander by.

Mountains rise in silent grace,
Marking trails of forgotten lore.
In the wanderer's tranquil pace,
The world becomes forevermore.

The Eternal Silence

In the hush of twilight's fall,
Quiet reigns in twilight's veil.
Silence whispers through it all,
Stories spoken, without fail.

Stars above in silent gaze,
Witness to the world's deep pause.
In their light, a silent praise,
Breathless awe without a cause.

Moonlight floods the silent night,
Casting shadows long and deep.
In its glow, the world takes flight,
Into dreams, eternal sleep.

The Celestial Continuum

Stars whisper secrets in the night
Through a tapestry spun so bright
Galaxies weave tales afar
Ancient echoes from every star

Eternal rivers of cosmic light
Flowing softly through endless flight
In shadows, planets softly spin
Dreams of existence, deep within

Nebulas hum a mystic tune
Beneath the cradle of the moon
Asteroids drift through time and space
Witness to creation's embrace

Heavens stretch through boundless reach
Wisdom written for those who seek
In the continuum they gleam
Guardians of the cosmic dream

Infinite Oasis

An endless desert of golden hues
Beneath the sky's cerulean blues
Oasis whispers through the sand
Life's refuge in this arid land

Mirages dance on scorching waves
Secrets of past, what nature saves
Palms sway gently, a calming plea
Water glimmers in vast decree

In shadows cool, we seek repose
Where life's lifeblood softly flows
Echoes of a promise serene
Sheltered by the verdant green

Infinite under the desert skies
An oasis where the heart lies
A sanctuary, pure and free
Timeless in its tranquility

Sacred Eternity

In the stillness of the night
Under the moon's gentle light
Whispers of sacred tales unfold
In silence, mysteries retold

Eternity speaks in hushed tones
Through roots of ancient, weathered stones
In the heart a flame does burn
With every lesson, we discern

Time's embrace, a cosmic grace
Guiding us through boundless space
History's echoes call to thee
Threads that weave our sacred plea

In the cradle of the earth
Rebirth and death, a constant mirth
Eternity, our souls' delight
A ceaseless dance, both day and night

Ephemeral Immensity

The morning mist that fills the air
A fleeting dream, a passing stare
Moments dance on soft sunbeams
In the light, a thousand gleams

Mountains rise, grand and sublime
Guardians of the edge of time
Valleys whisper tales once known
In their shadow, seeds are sown

Sky and sea in vast embrace
Mirrors of a boundless space
Ephemeral winds, with gentle sighs
Carry whispers through the skies

Life's river flows, both wild and mild
Ephemeral notes, so freely styled
In immensity, we find our place
Transitory in endless grace

Endless Pathways

Through woods and over hills, I go
Where rivers twist and winds do blow
In search of dreams yet undefined
On pathways endless, soul aligned

Beneath the stars, I find my way
With night as guide and moon as ray
Each step I take, a silent quest
To seek the places love is blessed

No map nor compass do I need
For heart and soul are all the creed
In nature's arms, no bounds confine
On endless pathways, I am fine

The whispering leaves, the call of skies
In trails of green, my spirit flies
O wandering feet, with roots untied
On endless pathways, I abide

Beyond the Veil of Time

In shadows of the past, we tread
Where echoes of the old are spread
From ancient tales and lore sublime
We journey past the veil of time

A world unseen yet always near
Where whispered winds our souls endear
With every tick, with every chime
We glimpse beyond the veil of time

Eternal moments stitched in air
A tapestry beyond compare
The threads of life, both dark and prime
Are woven past the veil of time

So close your eyes and step inside
Where past and present both abide
In dreams and myth, in whispered rhyme
We live beyond the veil of time

Timeless Wonders

The cliffs that kiss the azure sky
Where eagles dare and clouds drift by
In ancient stones and waves that churn
Timeless wonders, vast and stern

Beneath the forest's emerald dome
Where silence speaks and shadows roam
The stories of the earth do turn
In timeless wonders, we discern

The sands of deserts, oceans wide
Where endless mysteries still hide
Each grain and wave, a lesson learned
Through timeless wonders, we're concerned

In every dawn and twilight's gleam
The echoes of a lasting dream
In nature's realm, our hearts intern
For timeless wonders still return

Infinite Silence

In quiet realms of thought I rest
Where noise and strife do not molest
A whispering hush, serene, intense
In realms of infinite silence

The murmurs of the ancient seas
The rustling leaves and sighing breeze
All blend into a sweet pretense
Of nature's infinite silence

No sound of clamor, no distress
Just tranquil moments, nothing less
In solitude, my soul dispense
To bask in infinite silence

Where thoughts do flow like placid streams
Unhindered by the rough extremes
In peaceful calm, my spirit's lens
Sees all through infinite silence

Illusions of the Eternal

Eternal dreams in moonlit glow
Fields where endless rivers flow
Beyond the stars, a secret gleam
A realm untouched by time's stream

Whispers dancing in the night
Shadows bathed in soft starlight
Visions fleeting, swiftly turn
Like embers in the heavens burn

In this realm, the soul finds flight
Boundless skies in velvet night
Echoes call from past and new
Threads of fate we barely knew

Timeless weave of night and day
Silent paths where hopes can stray
In the realm of dream and dawn
Eternity is gently drawn

Whispers Beyond the Horizon

A horizon kissed by sunlight's end
Whispers of where dreams ascend
Softly carried on twilight's breeze
Secrets beyond, among the trees

Gentle waves on distant shores
Of timeless tales and ancient lore
Stars aligned in cosmic dance
A wistful beckon, a fleeting chance

In quiet moments, hearts do yearn
For the hidden paths we learn
Beyond the reach of mortal grasp
Echoes in the silent clasp

The horizon's edge, a mystery
And whispers of what's yet to be
In shadowed dusk, the voices blend
Eternity begins to mend

Echoes of the Eternal

Echoes in the canyon deep
Songs that never seem to sleep
Winds of time that softly sigh
Carrying hints of ages nigh

Stars that shine in endless night
Guiding with their ancient light
Each a whisper, each a call
From the dawn to twilight's fall

Mountains hold the earth's deep song
In their shadow, weary long
Secrets locked in silent stone
Echoes of the world unknown

In the fabric, we are sewn
With the stars, we are not alone
Each echo in the timeless stream
Carries whispers of the dream

Timeless Reflections

Mirrored lakes of crystal clear
Reflections of the yesteryear
In their depths, the ages lie
Time's elusive lullaby

Silent ripples on the past
Moments cherished meant to last
Every wave a tale untold
Stories in the water rolled

Glimmered moon on silent pond
Of the memories we're fond
In reflections yet unseen
Lie the echoes of the dream

Through the years, reflection shows
Paths we took, and where time flows
In the timeless water's gleam
Lies the heart of every dream

Chasing Forever

Beneath the endless sky, we soar
With dreams that reach beyond the shore
Time slips through our eager grasp
Yet still, we chase what cannot last

Stars above, like ancient guides
Illuminate where future hides
Though fleeting as a morning dew
We chase the dreams we hold as true

Cross valleys wide, through tempests strong
We sing forever's hopeful song
Each step, a promise to the dawn
Though night may fall, we carry on

In whispered winds and silent night
We find the courage for the flight
And though forever's far away
We'll chase its gleam with each new day

Reflections of Eternity

In mirrored lakes, where silence dreams
Reflections speak in silvered streams
A timeless dance of light and shade
In memories, both bright and frayed

Eternity within a glance
A moment's pause, a fleeting chance
To see the past and future blend
In endless loops that have no end

The echo of a bygone sigh
In twilight's soft and gentle cry
A whisper of what once had been
And what, in time, we'll see again

As night unfolds its velvet gown
And stars in silent rows look down
We ponder all that's come to be
In quiet reflections of eternity

Cosmic Fragments

In the tapestry of night
Scattered gems of ancient light
Whisper tales of stars long gone
Cosmic fragments, journey drawn

Across the void, celestial paths
Mapping histories in their math
Each fragment holds a silent quest
A story told, a soul at rest

Galaxies in sacred dance
Bound by fate, not chance
A symphony of age-old lore
Beginnings gone, forevermore

Nebulae and constellations bright
Guardians of the endless night
In every spark, a life ignites
Cosmic fragments, timeless lights

Enduring Dreams

In painted hues of dawn's embrace
Dreams take flight, find their place
Enduring through the storm and strife
Echoes of a vibrant life

A whisper in the quiet dark
A glimmer, faint, a spark
Beneath the weight of endless seas
Dreams rise, they claim with ease

Through winding paths and shadowed glen
We hold our hopes within
A lantern in the deepest night
A beacon, fierce and bright

For dreams endure, they never fade
In heart and soul, they're made
And in their light, we find our way
Enduring dreams, our endless day

Tracing the Unending

In twilight's grasp, where shadows converge,
We trace the paths of endless surge.
Through time's vast sea, our spirits blend,
In whispers soft, the echoes send.

The stars align, a silent choir,
Guiding hearts through realms afire.
In dreams we find our way ahead,
Tracing the unending, where we're led.

Between the dawn and dusk we weave,
A tapestry of fate's reprieve.
Beyond the veil of night's embrace,
We journey forth in endless grace.

Through life's expanse, a fleeting rhyme,
We dance on threads of woven time.
In every breath, love's timeless theme,
Tracing the unending, in our dream.

Beyond the Horizon

A horizon frames the dreams untold,
Where skies meet earth in shades of gold.
The sun dips low, a fiery blaze,
Beyond the reach of mortal gaze.

Waves of azure bear the call,
To venture forth, heart and all.
Chasing dusk and dawn's embrace,
Beyond the horizon, we find our place.

Mountains rise to kiss the sky,
Echoing the reasons why.
To realms unknown, our souls take flight,
Beyond the edge of fading light.

Fields of green, a vast expanse,
Whisper of a secret dance.
In the distance, dreams arise,
Beyond the horizon, in our eyes.

Eternal Symphony

A symphony eternal plays,
In hearts attuned to endless days.
The music of the spheres above,
Resonates in timeless love.

Notes cascade, a cosmic stream,
Awaking life from boundless dream.
In melodies of yesteryears,
We find our hopes, confront our fears.

The echoes of a song divine,
Weave through the very strands of time.
In chords of light, the spirit hums,
Eternal symphony becomes.

Through changing seasons, lyrics blend,
Harmonies that never end.
In every age, the tune repeats,
Eternal symphony completes.

Timeless Illumination

In the silence of a dream-filled night,
The stars reveal their ancient light.
Timeless tales they softly weave,
In patterns vast, new minds conceive.

A lantern's glow in darkest hour,
Eternal flame of hidden power.
Guiding steps through shadows' veil,
Timeless illumination prevails.

Wisdom lives in whispered breeze,
Truths that lie in rustling leaves.
In every radiant beam we find,
The endless light of boundless mind.

Through ages past and yet to be,
Light transcends mortality.
With every dawn, a fresh creation,
Timeless in its illumination.

Timeless Murmurs

Beneath the ancient oak so tall,
Are whispers of a time long past.
Each leaf a story, each root a call,
Through moments fleeting, shadows cast.

In dawn's first light the murmurs rise,
A tale they weave of yore and might.
Their voices soft, yet strong, comprise,
The echoes of a lost twilight.

The brook beside will softly hum,
A song that blends past dreams, now still.
To days where hearts and minds succumb,
To murmurs of an ageless will.

The starlit sky reveals a lore,
Written in paths of astral light.
Where dreams abide and spirits soar,
In murmurs bound by endless night.

Eternal Glimpses

Through veils of time, in shadows cast,
Are glimpses of the infinite.
Where moments merge both slow and fast,
And secrets slumber in the night.

In moonlit meadows, whispers soft,
Recount the tales of ages gone.
Of worlds unseen and dreams aloft,
A dance eternal, dusk till dawn.

A fleeting glance, a transient thought,
Reflects the timeless, boundless sea.
In visions where the soul is caught,
Glimpses of eternity.

Each starry gleam, a distant past,
Unravels truths in silent drift.
Where future meets with shadows cast,
In glimpses of eternal shift.

Endless Realms

Across the span of boundless skies,
In realms where timeless rivers flow.
A land of dreams before us lies,
Where endless possibilities grow.

Each whisper there, a beacon bright,
To guide the traveler through the haze.
In realms embraced by purest light,
A journey through eternal days.

Mountains echo ages old,
Valleys hum a mystic tune.
Through endless realms where stories told,
Are woven by the stars and moon.

In labyrinths of thought and time,
The realms of endless wonder gleam.
Their call a soft, enchanting chime,
Inviting all to dare and dream.

Cosmic Whispers

In spaces vast where stars align,
The cosmos breathes a quiet song.
A whisper in the grand design,
That binds the night so deep and long.

Each galaxy, a note serene,
Composes symphonies of light.
In whispers from the in-between,
Of cosmic awe and voids of night.

Through crystal veils where comets surge,
The whispers speak of endless fates.
In cosmic realms where thoughts converge,
On paths of light the soul awaits.

A dance of stars, a whispered call,
Through nebulae and silent tides.
The cosmic whispers hold us all,
In their embrace, where truth abides.

Endless Horizons

Beyond the plains where shadows flee,
Where boundless skies meet endless sea,
A world untamed, where spirits soar,
Horizons call forevermore.

Mountains rise with silent grace,
Whispers lost in timeless space,
Stars above, a guiding light,
Through the vast and endless night.

Winds that sing through ancient trees,
Secrets held by mystic breeze,
Footprints fade on sands of gold,
Stories of the brave and bold.

In the dawn or twilight's gleam,
Chasing life's eternal dream,
Paths unknown and trails unseen,
Questing where our hearts have been.

Endless horizons far and wide,
Onward to the great divide,
Journey forth, embrace the call,
Forever seeking, standing tall.

Whispers of Eternity

In the silence of the night,
Whispers soft, a gentle light,
Echoes of the ages gone,
Bringing hope, till breaking dawn.

Through the veil where shadows play,
Hushed murmurs begin to sway,
Songs that time itself forgot,
Woven in a timeless knot.

Ancient tales by stars revealed,
In the wind, their secrets sealed,
Voices from forgotten lands,
Touching hearts with unseen hands.

In the dance of moonlit streams,
Dreams are born of endless dreams,
Whispers of eternity,
Guide us through infinity.

From the past to future's call,
Mysteries that bind us all,
Listen close, the soul's decree,
In the whispers, find the key.

The Unseen Realm

In mysteries the shadows lie,
An unseen world beyond the sky,
Hidden truths and secrets deep,
Where ancient dreams forever sleep.

Through the mist and twilight's hue,
Glimpses of a world anew,
Phantoms of the past arise,
In the unseen realm of skies.

Eyes that see what none have seen,
Wander through the in-between,
Silent steps on paths unknown,
In the realms where thoughts have flown.

Magic weaves its quiet thread,
Binding realms of living, dead,
Portals to a distant sphere,
Where every wish and hope are near.

In this space, time stands still,
Echoes of a distant thrill,
Journey through the mind's own helm,
To the vast, unseen realm.

Timeless Echoes

Within the halls of memory,
Timeless echoes whisper free,
Calling from the days of old,
Stories in the shadows told.

Reflections of the lives we've led,
Footsteps from the paths we tread,
Echoes that will never fade,
Woven by the dreams we've made.

In the silence, voices blend,
Choruses that never end,
Songs of joy and tales of sorrow,
Woven in a shared tomorrow.

Ancient rhythms touch the land,
Played by nature's gentle hand,
Echoes of the earth and sky,
Songs that never say goodbye.

Past and present intertwine,
Crafting stories so divine,
In the echoes, timeless found,
Spirits lift without a bound.

Eternal Reflections

In the mirror of the lake, clear as morning dew,
Sky and water blend, merging every hue.
Echoes of the past, in waves softly part,
Boundless and deep, whisper to the heart.

Under twilight's veil, stars begin to gleam,
Silent witnesses to every dream.
Ripples fade in time's unending flow,
Carrying ancient secrets, we may never know.

Gilded glimmers dance with the moon's soft rays,
Tracing the night with ephemeral displays.
An endless cycle of dusk and dawn,
Nature's endless canvas beautifully drawn.

Through ages untold, stories they keep,
Shores of memory, where the soul might sleep.
Eternal reflections, in every drop and glance,
Refractions of a timeless, serene romance.

The Limitless Beyond

Past the horizon where the eagles soar,
Lies a realm untouched, forever more.
Mountains whisper to the distant skies,
Questions linger, in silent cries.

Where the sun kisses the edge of the earth,
Infinite dreams abound, given birth.
Beyond the known, where shadows play,
Whispers promise another way.

Stars are lanterns in the cosmic sea,
Guiding thoughts to where they are free.
Eternal nights and endless dawns,
In the tapestry of time, one belongs.

Can we grasp the vast untamed? Yet,
The heart seeks what mind won't forget.
In the limitless beyond, we strive,
A quest where dreams and hopes both thrive.

Whispers in the Void

Between the stars, where darkness reigns,
A silent choir sings of ancient pains.
Ethereal echoes in the void, so vast,
Transcending time, both future and past.

Fleeting shadows, dancing without form,
In cosmic realms where silence is the norm.
Mystical voices whisper through the night,
Weave the fabric of the unseen sight.

Veiled whispers of what once was known,
In the silent void, forever alone.
Timeless tales in the dark abyss,
Unfold secrets that we may miss.

Beyond the edge of mortal thought,
Echoes of existence silently fought.
In the void, where light and darkness meet,
Eternal whispers of a cosmic beat.

Boundaries of the Unknowable

At the edge of comprehension and unseen lines,
Lies the realm where mystery entwines.
Shadows drift where light cannot chase,
Concealing truths in a hidden space.

Beyond the realm of eyes and reason,
Exist thoughts in an endless season.
Boundaries fade where logic is barred,
A dance of the heart, eternally scarred.

Through veils of mist, glimpses appear,
Of worlds unknown and futures dear.
The unknowable whispers in twilight tones,
Secrets carved in ancient stones.

The search for meaning in endless night,
Through corridors of secluded light.
Boundaries blurred, the quest renews,
In the unknowable, our souls peruse.

Fragments of Forever

In a moment, timeless, we abide,
Shadows dance, and secrets hide,
Fragments of forever lie,
In the corners of our eye.

Stars that hung in endless skies,
Glimmer now in your eyes,
Echoes of a distant past,
In this time, we hope to last.

Eternal whispers in the night,
Guide our souls through silent light,
Fragments fall, yet love will rise,
In the realm where truth lies.

In each breath, a story sown,
In each heart, the seeds are blown,
Forever's pieces, scattered wide,
In the universe, we confide.

Illimitable Dreams

In the web of night, we weave,
Dreams untold, we do believe,
Illimitable, our thoughts do soar,
Reaching out forevermore.

Through the clouds, beyond the sea,
Visions bloom in endless spree,
In each dawn a dream is born,
From the night, the veil is torn.

Mysteries entwine our path,
Winds of fate in silent wrath,
Dreams that stretch beyond the now,
To the stars, we make our vow.

Through the realms of ether glide,
With our dreams as sacred guide,
Illimitable, our hearts will gleam,
In the light of our shared dream.

Whispers of Never-ending

Silent voices fill the air,
In this place, beyond compare,
Whispers of a never-ending,
Through our hearts, they're gently sending.

Time and space may drift apart,
Yet our souls, they know the art,
Of embracing whispers' creed,
In the silent night, they lead.

Infinite, the tale unfolds,
In our hands, the truth it holds,
Whispers flow like streams unseen,
In our minds, they softly glean.

Everlasting, faint, they glide,
Through the space where we confide,
Never-ending, ever there,
In our dreams, they lay us bare.

Endless Echoes

Through the canyon, voices sound,
In the hearts, they are found,
Endless echoes, boundless roam,
In the silence, they find home.

Whispers carried through the years,
Melding joy and hidden fears,
Echoes of the ages past,
In the present, they will last.

Through the void, the echoes span,
Linking spirit, earth, and man,
Endless, timeless in their call,
Fading not, they bind us all.

In the stillness, echoes trace,
Lines of truth in every place,
Resonating through our lives,
Endless echoes, where love thrives.

Infinite Whispers

In the hush of twilight's sigh,
Where the dreams and shadows lie,
Whispers weave through realms unseen,
Hopes and fears in whispers keen.

In the void of endless night,
Stars wink secrets, soft and slight,
Echoes of what might have been,
Travel in the silent din.

A breeze breathes through ancient pines,
Tales of lost and hidden signs,
Murmurs touch the heart and mind,
Whispered truths—so hard to find.

From the past and future's blend,
To the whispers there, attend,
Without end, they speak and sing,
Infinite as dreams take wing.

Celestial Reflections

Mirror skies in dusk unveiled,
Cosmic dreams in folds entailed,
Stars like pearls in velvet spun,
Heaven's light from day begun.

A dance of shadows, light and dark,
Celestial echoes leave their mark,
Planets waltz through endless space,
In mirror's depth, we find our place.

Galaxies in ocean's reach,
Endless lessons, they do teach,
Reflections of the cosmic pane,
In our eyes, the vast domain.

With each turn of night's embrace,
Time is drawn within this space,
Reflections from the stars above,
Whisper stories, songs of love.

Eternal Patterns

Life's design in threads entwined,
Patterns of the heart and mind,
Cycles weave in endless flair,
In their dance, we live and wear.

Time's great loom through ages runs,
Crafts its art in moon and suns,
Patterns shroud our fleeting years,
In their shapes, our hopes and fears.

Mysteries in symbols wrought,
Etching tales and cryptic thought,
In the mind's unfathomed night,
Patterns gleam in hidden light.

Through the fabric, stretched and torn,
New designs reborn, reborn,
Eternal are these threads that craft,
Patterns held in cosmic draft.

Silhouettes of Eternity

Shadows cast by ancient light,
Silhouettes in dusk's soft flight,
Eternal forms on cosmic stage,
Writing tales on life's great page.

Figures etched in twilight's hue,
Boundless realms they wander through,
Ephemeral yet deeply true,
Timeless shades in endless view.

Histories in shadows trace,
Lineage of cosmic grace,
In their silent, spectral play,
Eternal moment, night and day.

Through the veil, they twist and bend,
Mark the journey, path, and end,
Silhouettes in twilight born,
Eternity in shadows worn.

The Eternal Canvas

Upon the sky's wide, boundless dome,
Where dreams and stars entwine.
Existence paints its endless poem,
In hues of dark and shine.

Each stroke a tale of silent grace,
Unfolding through the night.
The cosmos bares its tender face,
To hearts that seek its light.

A masterpiece with no refrain,
Yet songs of old are heard.
In whispers of the falling rain,
Soft murmurs of a word.

With every dawn, a new expanse,
Where hopes and fears are spun.
In the grand, eternal dance,
The canvas is begun.

As long as time and space persist,
Its beauty will be shown.
For in each heart, it does exist,
A realm that's never known.

Boundless Silence

In the quiet of the night,
Where shadows softly play.
There lies a world, concealed from sight,
In whispers of the day.

The silence speaks in muted tones,
Of mysteries profound.
In ancient, unseen monochromes,
Its secrets do resound.

Each echo tells a tale untold,
In silence, truth abides.
In stillness, wisdom does unfold,
And time itself confides.

Through boundless realms of quiet peace,
Where thoughts and dreams align.
The ceaseless waves of stillness cease,
In silence so divine.

The boundless silence, pure and vast,
A refuge for the mind.
Within its depths, we find at last,
The solace we confined.

Whispers of Forever

In the whispers of forever,
Where eternity is sown.
There lies a bond no force can sever,
In star-lit dreams, unknown.

Each moment bleeds into the next,
A river without end.
Life's fleeting murmurs, sweetly text,
In whispers that transcend.

A dance that spans the ages long,
With steps both bold and slight.
Where echoes of an ancient song,
Resound within our night.

The whispers tell of love and fear,
Of triumphs and regret.
In every beat, in every tear,
The eternal vows are set.

So listen close, and you shall hear,
A tale that never dies.
The whispers of forever, near,
Beneath the endless skies.

Beyond the End

Beyond the end, a realm unfolds,
Where night and day entwine.
A tapestry of tales retold,
In whispers soft, divine.

The shadows cast by dying stars,
Illuminate the way.
To lands untouched by worldly scars,
Where time and space decay.

In twilight's glow, the path extends,
To dreams that never cease.
Where echoes of the journey blend,
To form a timeless peace.

The end is but a door ajar,
A gateway to the new.
Where souls are free to wander far,
Beyond the earthly view.

So fear not what the end may bring,
For there, the heart ascends.
To realms where boundless spirits sing,
In love, beyond the end.

Whispers of Cosmos

In the silence of night, stars entwine,
Softly they sing, a celestial sign.
Galaxies dance in a silent embrace,
Echoes of time in endless space.

Nebulae whisper secrets untold,
Mysteries of space, ancient and old.
Planets spin in their eternal flight,
Mirrors of dreams in the abyss of night.

Comets blaze through the darkened sky,
Tales of wonder as they pass by.
The universe breathes in a symphony,
Choreographed in cosmic harmony.

Each constellation, a story unfold,
Of love, loss, and wisdom from ages cold.
Beneath this vast expanse, we lie,
Traders of dreams, voyagers through the sky.

And as I gaze upon the cosmic sea,
I hear whispers beckoning to me.
In the heart of the cosmos, far and near,
Lie answers to questions we hold dear.

Boundless Horizons

Beyond the hills where the sun does rise,
Lies a realm of endless skies.
Mountains kiss the heavens high,
Dreams take wing, and spirits fly.

Oceans vast and rivers wide,
Chasing horizons, where dreams reside.
Each wave a whisper, guiding the way,
Towards tomorrows, born from today.

In fields of gold and forests deep,
Secrets of the earth do sleep.
Boundless horizons, a call to roam,
Every path leads us closer to home.

Canyons carved by waters flow,
Etching stories of long ago.
With every step, we leave a trace,
Mapping journeys in time and space.

Skies ablaze with twilight hues,
Canvas of dreams, in vibrant clues.
Boundless horizons, ever near,
Inviting us to wonder without fear.

The Unseen Path

Through the woods, where shadows play,
Lies an unseen path, inviting way.
Whispers of leaves underfoot,
Guiding hearts where dreams took root.

Mist hangs low, a silken veil,
Mysteries woven in each trail.
Steps uncharted, a journey unplanned,
Finding magic in the touch of land.

Rays of sun through canopies break,
Illuminating paths we make.
In the unknown, courage grows,
With every turn, a new hope sows.

Echoes of ancients fill the air,
Guiding those who wander there.
Each stone a story, each branch a guide,
Trust the path where secrets hide.

In the silence, a whisper clear,
The unseen path draws ever near.
With open heart and fearless mind,
We discover treasures left behind.

Endless Possibilities

In the dawn of a brand new day,
Endless possibilities light our way.
Horizons gleam with promise bright,
Dreams unfurl in morning's light.

Paths untraveled, futures unknown,
Seeds of potential we have sown.
Every step, a chance to see,
What magic lies in destiny.

Stars align and chaos bends,
In our hands, the power of amends.
Limitless pathways stretched before,
Each breath a key to open more.

With courage bold and hearts ablaze,
We navigate life's winding maze.
Endless possibilities at our feet,
Every heartbeat, a chance to meet.

In every failure, a spark anew,
Lessons learned, and avenues too.
Embrace the journey with open eyes,
For in endless possibilities, freedom lies.

Unbounded Echoes

Within the realms of shattered dreams,
A whisper floats on silent streams.
Unseen yet loud in hidden cores,
It dances through forgotten doors.

Voices from the past entwine,
In twilight's soft, ephemeral shine.
Echoes trace the time-worn path,
Leaving shadows in their aftermath.

Memories weave through cryptic tunes,
Beneath the watch of pale-faced moons.
Ancient whispers pierce the night,
Grains of time take flight.

Haunting calls in forests deep,
Where secrets of the night shall keep.
Resonance in endless bounds,
In the heart, its beat resounds.

Eternal Silhouettes

Beneath the sky's eternal dome,
Figures roam where shadows roam.
Their outlines etched in twilight's grace,
Timeless forms in empty space.

Specters of a bygone age,
Written on the night's dark page.
Silhouettes of love and war,
Stories locked in silent lore.

Ghostly frames on the horizon's edge,
Their presence but a whispered pledge.
Bound by night, yet free by day,
In the mists, they slowly sway.

Endless twilight, they embark,
Waltzing past the tired lark.
Through the void they softly tread,
Eternal shades of what once bled.

Boundless Visions

In realms where dreams are left to sprawl,
Visions break through shadow's thrall.
To worlds where wonders never cease,
And hearts find everlasting peace.

Boundless canvases, bright and vast,
Painted with the hues of past.
Future fades into the now,
Dreamers take an endless bow.

Horizons stretch beyond the stars,
Unseen realms, they bear no bars.
Infinite hues, cascading light,
Unfolding scenes in pure delight.

Within the mind's expansive maze,
Visions spark and endlessly blaze.
Pure and wild, forever free,
In the boundless, we shall be.

Endless Fragments

Scattered pieces in the wind,
Tales begin and never end.
Fragments of what once was whole,
Whispers of a distant goal.

Memories in shards collide,
On the waves of time they ride.
Each a light in darkened sky,
Endless echoes, no goodbye.

Splinters wrapped in golden dreams,
In the silence, gently gleams.
Pieces of an ancient lore,
Dancing through each open door.

Through the mists of time and space,
Fragments of a boundless grace.
Boundless yet they stay confined,
Endless in the seeker's mind.

The Uncharted Immensity

Vast oceans stretch, untouched and wide,
Dreams of the brave, where secrets hide.
Whispers of winds, on waves they glide,
A mystic call, a calming tide.

Beyond the stars, and realms unknown,
Legends lived, and stories grown.
Heartbeats echo, not alone,
In depths where seeds of hope are sown.

Mountains rise with silent grace,
Kissed by sun's first warm embrace.
Echoes sing in quiet space,
Of time's unyielding, endless chase.

Skies aflame with twilight's glow,
Horizons where adventures flow.
Paths untrod and journeys slow,
In realms where wild dreams may grow.

The uncharted waits for those who seek,
In valleys vast and summits peak.
In every venture, wisdom speak,
The language only brave hearts speak.

Fragments of the Endless

In shards of time, a puzzle stays,
Of ancient nights and fleeting days.
Silent whispers, mystic ways,
Of endless light and shadowed maze.

Pieces scattered, stars aflight,
Through veils of moon and cosmic night.
Wonders hidden, out of sight,
In distant echoes of twilight.

Mirror's edge where truths collide,
Reflections of the worlds inside.
In every fragment, dreams reside,
Of endless seas and shifting tide.

Winds of change in whispered tones,
Guide the heart where mystery roams.
In fragments, life's sweet overtones,
In echoed love, the soul intones.

Through time's fabric, lines entwine,
Of endless forms, both bold and fine.
In fragments, endless truths define,
The dance of stars in grand design.

Twilight of Perpetuity

The sun descends, a golden hue,
Bidding day its soft adieu.
In twilight's grasp, time feels anew,
Whispers of eternity's view.

Shadows stretch, and stars ignite,
In canvas vast of purest light.
Echoes form in silent night,
A serenade of time's flight.

Colors blend in soft caress,
Of days gone by, their gentleness.
In twilight's arms, we find redress,
A moment's peace, a sweet recess.

Silhouettes of dreams long past,
In twilight's glow, forever cast.
Eternity's song, a melody vast,
Of moments fleeting, but meant to last.

As night unfolds, the world's embrace,
Time stands still in twilight's trace.
In boundless skies, we find our place,
A whisper of perpetual grace.

Spaces of the Infinite

In gaps between the silent stars,
Lie echoes of the distant spars.
Mysteries held in astral jars,
Of endless skies and cosmic scars.

Infinite realms where dreams reside,
In spaces where new worlds abide.
Wonders vast and journeys wide,
In timeless dance, time's gentle tide.

Galaxies weave through endless night,
In spaces vast, in boundless flight.
Nebulous dreams in rays of light,
The tapestry of cosmic sight.

Each thought a star in mind's expanse,
In infinite's ever-changing dance.
Questions formed as moments glance,
In worlds unknown, we find our chance.

The infinite calls in silent song,
To hearts that yearn, to spirits strong.
In spaces deep where we belong,
A journey's end, yet ever long.

Boundless Echoes

Through endless halls where dreams align,
Whispers drift in soft design,
Shadows play, entwine the scenes,
Lost within life's shifting streams.

Celestial tunes in starlit night,
Guide us through the fading light,
Memory's chords, a lonesome flute,
Echoes whisper, then are mute.

Journey far on whispers' wings,
Timeless tales the silence brings,
Round and round the echoes chime,
Dancing through the threads of time.

Voices weave and carry on,
In the dusk before the dawn,
Harmonies in distant lands,
Echoes drawn in shifting sands.

Endless echoes, never still,
Call us from the distant hill,
In their song we find our place,
Boundless in the vast embrace.

The Everlasting Dance

In the meadow's gentle sway,
Where the golden sunbeams play,
Spirits waltz in endless trance,
Caught within the ancient dance.

Moonlight casts its silver veil,
Over fields that softly pale,
Steps in rhythm, hearts in tune,
Mingling 'neath the quiet moon.

Hands entwine in twilight's glow,
Round and round the dancers go,
Footsteps light on dewy grass,
Every moment soon shall pass.

Stars above serve as their guide,
Through the night they slip and glide,
Graceful forms in endless seven,
Silent songs of earth and heaven.

In this dance that never ends,
Boundless joy and sorrow blend,
Every heartbeat, every chance,
Found within the endless dance.

Timeless Reveries

In the quiet of the dawn,
Dreams arise and shadows gone,
Waking whispers, soft as breeze,
Timeless are the reveries.

Thoughts adrift on seas of calm,
Rest within a soulful psalm,
Cradled in a dreamer's sigh,
Never does the moment die.

Eyes that gaze upon the hue,
Of a sky that's ever new,
Time dissolves in this embrace,
Of an ever-changing face.

Memories in soft refrain,
Echo through the heart's domain,
Each a story, each a song,
Lingering as time moves on.

In the realms of endless nights,
Where the mind in silence flights,
There we find our secret seas,
In these timeless reveries.

Infinite Shadows

In the twilight's gentle clasp,
Shadows flit and shadows grasp,
Whispers of the night unbound,
In their dance no sound is found.

Silken shades beneath the trees,
Swaying in the midnight breeze,
Phantom forms that come and go,
Woven in the moonlight's glow.

Across the fields and silent streams,
Run the threads of shadowed dreams,
Infinite and ever near,
Yet dissolving into clear.

Mysteries the night unfolds,
In the dark their stories told,
Silent seers of worlds unseen,
Cast by light in silver sheen.

Where they wander none can know,
Silent steps in ebb and flow,
Boundless are these spectral shows,
In the realm of infinite shadows.

Unseen Eternity

In shadows deep, beyond the veil,
Whispers of worlds yet to unveil,
Secrets hidden, stars concealed,
An endless realm, fate unrevealed.

Time stands still, no dawn, no dusk,
Infinity's breath, a subtle musk,
Waves of silence, oceans vast,
The present fades, the futures cast.

Between the stars, where spirits tread,
Voices echo, the unsaid,
In twilight's glow, dreams ascend,
A boundless journey, never end.

Mystery's shroud, darkness bright,
Eternal realms, beyond sight,
An unseen pulse, a silent beat,
Eternity's dance, forever fleet.

A hopeful whisper, a gentle sigh,
In endless night, the soul will fly,
Through cosmic realms, unknown, unseen,
In eternity's embrace, serene.

Celestial Horizons

Beyond the hills, where skies expand,
Lies a realm, both grand and grand,
Stars like jewels, night's tapestry,
The universe whispers, wild and free.

Lift your gaze, where dreams reside,
Celestial realms, horizons wide,
Galaxies weave, a cosmic tale,
A beacon bright, beyond the pale.

In the dome of night, vast and clear,
Mysteries dance without a fear,
Planets spin, in harmony,
The dance of time, eternity.

Constellations trace ancient lore,
Silent tales of what's come before,
Light years traverse, unfathomed span,
The universe holds secrets of man.

With every dawn, new light unveils,
Horizons whisper, endless trails,
In the vast expanse, dreams converge,
On celestial paths, souls emerge.

The Infinite Dance

In the cosmic ballroom, stars align,
Galaxies swirl, a dance divine,
Nebulae waltz, in silken light,
Infinity's heartbeat, pure delight.

Planets twirl, in rhythmic grace,
Across the void, an endless space,
Moons in orbit, silent glide,
In the dance of time, side by side.

Comets streak, a fiery trail,
In this astral harmony, none frail,
Black holes spin, a phantom's trance,
In the universe's infinite dance.

Celestial bodies, vast and grand,
In this ballet, perfectly planned,
Eternal choreography, so profound,
In the dance of life, we are bound.

Every heartbeat, a stellar beat,
Every soul, a rhythm so sweet,
In the cosmos, we find our chance,
To join in the infinite dance.

Timeless Mirrors

In ancient glass, reflections gleam,
Timeless tales, within they teem,
Echoes of past, whispers of now,
Time's continuum, in mirrors vow.

Glimpses of yesteryears reside,
In reflections, truths are bide,
Future's shimmer, faintly seen,
Timeless mirrors, ever keen.

Each gaze in the silent pane,
Shows a life's fleeting refrain,
In mirrored realms, shadows blend,
Time's illusion, without end.

Silvered glass, a seer's eye,
Through which memories can't lie,
A reflection of what might be,
Timeless mirrors, eternally free.

Gaze within, find wisdom's light,
In reflections, day and night,
Mirrors hold the ever true,
Timeless as the sky is blue.

Eternal Cascade

In misty veils the river flows,
Through valleys deep where secrets grow.
Whispers from the ancient foam,
Guiding onward, ever home.

Mountains bow to passing streams,
Reflecting all our distant dreams.
In nature's dance we find our place,
Caught within the cascade's grace.

Each droplet tells a timeless tale,
In every wave, an endless trail.
Journey through the ageless land,
Holding stardust in our hand.

With every turn, the waters sing,
Of life's eternal, endless ring.
Boundless currents weave our fate,
In the cascade, we relate.

The river's heart, a pulsing light,
Carries us beyond the night.
In its embrace, we're unafraid,
Lost within the cascade's shade.

Vistas of the Unending

Beyond the hills, where sky meets sea,
A world unfolds for you and me.
Infinite paths to wander free,
In the vistas of our destiny.

Colors blend, horizons wide,
Promises of dreams collide.
In every breeze, a whisper found,
In these vistas, we are unbound.

Eternal skies with stars alight,
Guiding travelers through the night.
Endless fields where hopes reside,
In these vistas, we confide.

Mountains rise with peaks so grand,
Touching realms beyond our hand.
In every shadow, mystery lies,
In these vistas, hearts arise.

With open hearts and eager sight,
We venture forth into the light.
Bound by nothing, spirits ascending,
In the vistas, unending.

The Vast Expanse

Horizons stretch where eyes can't see,
An endless realm of mystery.
In every breeze and mountain range,
The vast expanse, so wild and strange.

Fields of gold and forests deep,
Secrets in their silence keep.
Through every dawn and twilight's dance,
We walk the path of vast expanse.

Stars that guide the wanderer's way,
Night's canopy of vast display.
In every glimmer, dreams enhance,
Touched by the vast expanse.

Rivers carve their ageless flow,
Marking time in undertow.
In every wave, life's true romance,
Reflected in the vast expanse.

With open arms, we embrace the call,
Boundless, free, and standing tall.
In every step, a new advance,
Together, in the vast expanse.

Timeless Embers

In the hearth of ancient lore,
Timeless embers burn once more.
Whispered tales of days of yore,
Echo through the ages' core.

Flames that dance with gentle grace,
Casting light on every face.
Stories told by glowing fire,
Reflecting hearts and souls' desire.

In the quiet, embers glow,
Secrets from the past they show.
In their warmth, our spirits blend,
Timeless ties that never end.

Flickering lights in darkened night,
Guiding souls with gentle light.
In their dance, our dreams confer,
Watching timeless embers stir.

Gathered close, we watch and learn,
From the fires, we discern.
In every spark, a life's endeavour,
Held within timeless embers, forever.

Echoes in the Cosmos

Stars whisper tales of ancient light,
Orbiting through the velvet night.
Comets blaze with transient breath,
Marking trails in cosmic death.

Galaxies swirl in cosmic song,
Their melodies both fierce and long.
Nebulas paint with mystic hues,
In stellar dawns and twilight views.

Planets dance in orbital grace,
Round suns in a silent space.
Moons reflect with borrowed glow,
In endless tides that flux and flow.

Black holes whisper dark regime,
In voids where no light can beam.
Yet even in such shadow's clutch,
Echoes of creation still touch.

Across the span, the cosmos hums,
With secrets hidden in its drums.
For all who gaze and contemplate,
Echoes in the cosmos await.

Ethereal Pathways

Through forests deep with whispers low,
Where moonlight bathes in gentle glow,
Pathways edged with silver mist,
Lead to realms where faeries tryst.

Moss-clad stones and ancient trees,
Guard the secret, mystic keys.
Wisps of light dance in the breeze,
Echoes of lost memories.

From shadowed bends to crystal streams,
Pathways lead to land of dreams.
Veils of twilight, rustling leaves,
Hint of magic one perceives.

Every step on paths unseen,
Glimmers of true worlds serene.
Beyond the bridge of time's expanse,
Lies the realm where spirits dance.

Ethereal pathways wind and twist,
In moonlit mist, they quietly exist.
For those who seek and journey far,
They'll find their way by inner star.

Timeless Waltz

In mirrored halls of ancient lore,
Where time's patterns gently pour,
Figures dance in shadows light,
A waltz transcending day and night.

Step by step in measured grace,
They glide through epochs we can't trace.
Eternal music softly plays,
On strings of past and future days.

Each partner's touch, both firm and light,
Guides through the ebbing depth of night.
An ageless bond, they tightly keep,
As moments pass and centuries sleep.

Gowns of stardust, suits of space,
Twirl in a warm, embracing chase.
Timeless waltz in endless court,
Where cosmic dreams and time consort.

Echoes linger in the air,
Of waltzing steps beyond compare.
In that dance, time finds its pause,
Bound in love's undying cause.

Odyssey to the Eternal

Across the seas of time and space,
Voyagers seek an ageless place.
With hearts afire, spirits set,
On paths unknown their feet are met.

Through galaxies of swirling stars,
Past the realms where Neptune spars,
They chase the thread of distant lore,
From the epochs gone before.

Onward through the cosmic veil,
Where nebulae in hues unflail,
They journey to eternal gleam,
Beyond the bounds of thought and dream.

Each moment, timeless in their quest,
Through voids, they find their transient rest.
Celestial maps, they still unfold,
To find the mythic age of gold.

Odyssey to the eternal shore,
Where dreams reside, and spirits soar.
For those who dare the astral sea,
Eternity is their decree.

Infinite Reflections

In mirrors deep and clear
Worlds within worlds appear
Echoes of skies so near
Truths in each shimmered sphere

Light dances through the glass
Moments both slow and fast
Timeless yet sure to pass
Life's endless looking-glass

Each face a hidden tale
Through silvered seas we sail
Dreams in the moonlight pale
Stars trace our secret trail

Eyes meet and intertwine
Thoughts in a ghostly line
Each glance a silent sign
Forever to redefine

In silent reverie's glow
A universe we know
In mirrors, thoughts do flow
To distant realms we go

Eternal Pathways

Through woods of ancient lore
We tread a path before
Footfalls on earthen floor
To memories once more

Beneath the twilight's shade
Where fading light has strayed
Stories in twilight laid
Whispers from night conveyed

With every step we find
Fragments of past unwind
Threads of a fate entwined
In echoes left behind

The journey never ends
With every turn, it bends
Time's tapestry extends
Through sunsets, paths, and friends

Under the midnight sky
Where countless spirits fly
Paths to forever lie
In endless dreams we try

Limitless Glimpses

Through fleeting moments caught
In webs of dreams we're taught
Glimpses of what is sought
Beyond the bounds of thought

In visions wild and free
Across a boundless sea
Wonders await to be
Unseen yet there to see

Through each horizon's frame
Stars spell a secret name
Life's ever-burning flame
No two glimpses the same

Beneath the moon's soft crest
Where stardust comes to rest
Heartbeats in silence quest
For dreams within the breast

In flickers of the night
We chase the morning light
In glimpses pure and bright
Through endless skies in flight

The Unending Voyage

Set sail on azure streams
Through constellations' beams
On waves of golden dreams
The voyage never seems

With every crest and fall
Horizons cast their call
Endlessness one and all
In whispers rise and sprawl

Through tempests wild we roam
Seek shores to call our home
With stars as our regnome
In boundless space we comb

Each daybreak paints anew
A journey's boundless view
In skies of endless blue
We chase the morning dew

As twilight draws its veil
Our hearts set forth to sail
Through realms that never pale
The unending voyage tale

Timeless Shadows

In the quiet of the night,
Where time seems to pause,
Shadows whisper ancient secrets,
Of forgotten cause.

Through the veil of dreams,
They silently glide,
Hold secrets of the ages,
In them, truths confide.

Every corner darkened realm,
Hides stories of old,
Timeless whispers echoing,
Their mysteries unfold.

In shadows' silent embrace,
Memories swell,
Timeless, yet forever,
In the dark, they dwell.

Hear the echoes clearly,
In the stillness, hark,
Timeless shadows whisper,
Secrets in the dark.

Unending Horizons

Over hills and valleys,
Beyond what eyes can see,
Lie unending horizons,
Calling out to me.

Skies ablaze with color,
Touch the realms of gold,
Whispers of the morning,
Stories yet untold.

Winds that pass through meadows,
Kiss each blade with glee,
Tell of far-off places,
And lands wild and free.

Journey vast and boundless,
This path of light and blue,
Unending horizons,
Lure the heart that's true.

Endless as the ocean,
Or stars that brightly gleam,
Unending are the horizons,
In the wanderer's dream.

Beyond the Stars

Far beyond the twinkling,
Of the night sky's light,
Lie worlds of untold magic,
Hidden from our sight.

Galaxies in splendor,
Mark the cosmic chart,
Dreams of endless wonder,
Ignite the yearning heart.

Constellations whisper,
Tales of far-off lands,
Of realms beyond the stars,
Guided by unknown hands.

Each star a blazing beacon,
In the velvet dome,
Marking paths of wanderers,
On their stellar roam.

Beyond the stars, the secrets,
Of the universe dance,
A song of endless beauty,
In the cosmic expanse.

Echoes of Eternity

In the still of silence,
Where whispers gently lie,
Hear the echoes of eternity,
softly passing by.

Through the halls of ages,
Where ancients still reside,
Echoes whisper secrets,
Of the time and tide.

On the wings of stardust,
Carried by the breeze,
Timeless echoes murmur,
Through the endless seas.

In the quiet moments,
Listen with the heart,
You'll hear the echoes clearly,
As they gently start.

These echoes of eternity,
Bridge the then and now,
In their subtle resonance,
Time and space allow.

Fathomless Ventures

Beneath the azure seas we sail,
Through currents swift and veils of mist,
Chasing dreams on a quest so frail,
Where countless stars and oceans twist.

Each wave a tale of worlds untold,
Down the depths where shadows play,
Among the corals, secret gold,
In realms where endless sirens sway.

Compass lost but spirits high,
Voyagers of the sky and deep,
Charting paths where whispers lie,
In moonlit waters, secrets sleep.

Our hearts the only north we heed,
Drifting through the fathoms cold,
In search of truths that time has freed,
To grasp the light in stories bold.

Horizons widen, hearts expand,
Boundless ventures, hand in hand,
Together, through the storms we wade,
Until the dawn breaks night's cascade.

Eternity's Canvas

Brushstrokes of twilight paint the sky,
Where suns and moons in color blend,
On this vast canvas, dreams defy,
The boundaries where eternities end.

Whispering winds invoke the muse,
In fields where time and nature meet,
Their gentle hands the hues infuse,
With echoes of life's rhythmic beat.

A tapestry of age and grace,
Woven through nights of starlit song,
Each galaxy a fleeting trace,
In the grand expanse where moments throng.

Fleeting shadows, lights reborn,
Within this boundless, endless sprawl,
We leave our marks as day transforms,
In time's embrace, we rise, we fall.

Eternity, a living art,
Unbound by frames or mortal bind,
Each heartbeat a creative part,
In the vast expanse of space and mind.

The Perennial Quest

Through forests dense and valleys deep,
Across the peaks where eagles soar,
The quest for truth in silence seep,
Through ancient lands and myths of yore.

Each footstep paves a path anew,
In search of knowledge, life's great boon,
Where rivers sing and skies are blue,
Beneath the blazing sun and moon.

Whispers of the past we hear,
In echoes soft, the legend's lore,
Guiding us through doubt and fear,
Toward the light, forevermore.

Bound by wonder, free from strife,
We wander through both night and day,
In search of secrets paving life,
The ageless quest molds our sway.

With hearts as maps and minds aglow,
The journey's end not ours to see,
For in pursuit, our spirits grow,
Through timeless paths of mystery.

Timeless Filigree

In patterns fine, the seasons weave,
A filigree both pure and grand,
Time's tender touch in webs we leave,
With gentle art, by nature's hand.

Spring's blossom gently does unfurl,
In delicate threads of green and gold,
Life's fragile lace in every pearl,
In stories crafted, new and old.

Summer's rays with fervor kiss,
Etching warmth through leaf and field,
A golden braid in gentle bliss,
With radiant splendor, truths revealed.

Autumn's hues cascade like flames,
In vibrant strokes, the cycles spin,
Nature's tapestry reclaims,
The intricate weavings deep within.

In winter's calm, the silver weaves,
A tapestry of frost and dream,
On branches bare, where silence breathes,
Time's endless filigree supreme.

Boundless Horizons

Under the skies where dreams unfold,
Horizons stretch in hues of gold,
Infinite vistas, tales untold,
Across the world, we're brave and bold.

Mountains rise with peaks so high,
In fields of green, our spirits fly,
Through restless waves where currents lie,
We chase the clouds amidst the sky.

Endless paths where shadows play,
Each dawn brings light to guide the way,
In every step, in night and day,
We find our place, come what may.

The journey's long, yet here we stand,
With hopes and dreams in every hand,
Together we will roam the land,
United by a vision grand.

With hearts entwined, we face the rise,
Beyond the edge, to fullest skies,
Boundless horizons, our souls' prize,
Together we transcend all ties.

Cosmic Impressions

Starry nights, the heavens gleam,
Where worlds collide in cosmic dream,
The milky way, a timeless stream,
In twilight's glow, we find our theme.

Galaxies spin in endless dance,
Nebulae swirl in whispered trance,
With every star, we take a chance,
To glimpse beyond at night's expanse.

Planets drift in silent orbits,
Comets trail their fire-lit bits,
Through darkened voids, in astral splits,
The universe, a tapestry knits.

Patterns formed in stardust's light,
Constellations meet our sight,
In cosmic tales of day and night,
We seek the stars, our guiding light.

In endless space, our minds expand,
Among the stars, we find our stand,
Cosmic impressions, visions grand,
In the universe's open hand.

The Unending Journey

On roads unknown, where futures roam,
Through valleys deep and skies of dome,
We travel far from hearth and home,
Forever bound by dreams that foam.

With every mile, new tales arise,
In moonlit nights and dawning skies,
The horizon calls, an endless prize,
Our path ahead through lows and highs.

Each step we take, an echoed beat,
In desert sands or city street,
New faces met, new friendships greet,
The journey's pulse, our hearts repeat.

Through storm and sun, in wind and rain,
We push ahead, defy the strain,
Every loss and every gain,
Carved in memory's lasting chain.

No end in sight, the road extends,
With every turn, our spirit mends,
The unending journey, paths and bends,
Where every step, a story blends.

Endless Canvas

In fields of green and skies of blue,
We paint our dreams in every hue,
A canvas wide, both old and new,
With every stroke, the world we view.

Mountains high and oceans deep,
In colors bold, our fates we keep,
Through night and day, awake, asleep,
The endless canvas, memories seep.

With brushes fine, our hearts create,
In moments small and times of fate,
Each line a journey, path or gate,
A tapestry, intricate and great.

In shadows dark and lightened gleam,
We craft our hopes, our every dream,
In whispers soft or joyous scream,
The endless canvas, life's grand scheme.

Together we shall stand and paint,
With love as pure as any saint,
The endless canvas, bright and quaint,
Where life and art forever taint.

Milton Keynes UK
Ingram Content Group UK Ltd.
UKHW022156290524
443431UK00013B/315